NIALL ROTHN

Unknown Bath

Secrets and Scandals
from the Past

CARTOONS BY
FRASER MAY

ASHGROVE PRESS, BATH

Contents

A map locating the stories will be found on pages 40 and 41

Acknowledgments

The author would like to thank Miss F. Jones for typing his manuscript and Mr A. Dalton for photographing items from the Bath Reference Library.

The author and publishers gratefully acknowledge the permission of the Bath Reference Library to reproduce the photographs in items 3, 16, 18 and 21.

The publishers thank Martyn James for taking the photographs in items 1, 2, 6, 11, 13, 15 and 20.

Introduction

The general outline of Bath's history is well-known. Traditionally founded by Bladud, the city first came to prominence in the Roman period. After something of a decline in the Middle Ages it attracted the public again under the Tudors and Stuarts. In the 18th Century Richard 'Beau' Nash made it the most fashionable spa in the country and Wood and others built the squares and crescents for which Bath is still famous. Bath never quite recovered this sense of excitement again and soon settled down with a more respectable image. In this century the main event has been the bombing of Bath in World War II, causing widespread destruction and, in part, leading to the often controversial rebuilding of the last thirty years.

So at least runs the traditional account; but not all that has happened in Bath has necessarily appeared in the guide books . . .

The King's Bath

1. A Cure For All Ills?

For centuries people have been coming to Bath to take the waters as a cure for a large variety of ailments. As early as 1250 it was claimed that Bath's waters could cure leprosy. Later it was claimed they could help relieve indigestion and gout. The waters could ease limbs affected by rheumatism and palsy: grateful patients, once cured, would leave their crutches and sticks hanging as trophies on the walls of the baths. They cured all manner of skin diseases. On less reliable grounds, they also cured sterility: a succession of royal ladies came to Bath to produce heirs to the throne. Finally, even problems like obesity, deafness and forgetfulness could be helped by a course of the waters. In fact, despite many, many claims and investigations, there is precious little hard evidence to suggest why a great deal of warm water with traces of various minerals should be good for you.

There were two ways to take the waters: swimming in them and drinking them. Pepys, the famous diarist, was only one of many who took the first course. To modern eyes his routine might seem rather excessive. He arose at 4.00 a.m. to spend two hours immersed in the waters. Some doctors did question this practice. The baths were none too clean: the popular King's Bath was only mucked out twice a week. It was also open to the sky. If a gale was blowing, or if it was rainy, the only protection was a series of small niches in the walls. Non-medical critics were divided on why this activity should be frowned upon. Some said it inflamed the passions. In the 17th Century the practice of mixed nude bathing had been eventually stamped out but the linen bathing costumes used later did tend to cling rather too tightly to the body when wet. The relaxed and informal atmosphere brought many complaints of 'celebrated beauties, panting breasts and curious shapes, almost exposed to view.'

Far more people complained how unpleasant the baths were. The smell of sulphur and clouds of steam that met you as you entered the baths reminded many people of hell or, at least, purgatory. Smollett, the writer, hated the conditions and the 'chaos of the baths.' The combination of the heat and steam assaulted you, causing you to sweat profusely and have red streaming eyes. Smollett was also a little unsure of the water, especially as it stained your bathing clothes brown. Other hazards included the musicians who serenaded the bathers from above. Too many of the bathers sang along with the group and eventually they had to be removed. Some smoked tobacco while bathing. One play of the time features a character whose main source of fun was to enter the King's Bath naked and jump on the backs of both men and women to beat a tattoo.

The worst danger came from above. In the 16th and 17th Centuries high buildings and balconies surrounded the King's Bath and attracted many onlookers. Servants who came to fill bottles for their masters were apt to throw things at the bathers. Idlers threw small coins into the water for naked boys to dive after. Local hooligans threw each other in. Dogs, cats and pigs also went over the walls and into the bath. Wood likened it to a beer-garden. Charles I's wife, Henrietta Maria, when advised to visit a spa, preferred to go all the way to France rather then face the unruly elements at similar establishments in this country.

Not surprisingly, the idea grew that immersion in the water was not essential. Drinking it might be just as beneficial. One of the first to suggest this was Charles II's personal physician, Sir Alexander Fraser (the King paid a number of visits to Bath although rarely with the same woman). The cure was still rather excessive. Most doctors recommended drinking at least ten pints a day: not too quickly or you would spend too much time in the toilet. Nor should you indulge in strenuous exercise or all the beneficial value would be sweated off. Clearly it was important to keep the water inside you as long as possible. Even this activity held its dangers, though: for a long time there was no pump room and hardened patients had to stand around at open fountains, buffeted by the elements.

Why then did people think the waters did them good?

6

Sometimes cures can help if the patient merely thinks that they are useful, but the waters could also do some good, if by indirect methods. In past centuries clothes were not washed often; nor was the human body. Indeed many felt that an interest in hygiene was positively unhealthy; so swimming in the waters at least made sure that you had a wash and dry or diseased skin might be washed off. As for indigestion and over-indulgence, the system at least got a rest if you spent all day drinking nothing but water. This cure did not always work as intended. One 'bon viveur' arrived in Bath with severe gout and an over-worked stomach after living for years on a daily diet of a full three meals and a whole bottle of port. The doctors recommended he take the waters. He did, but they merely increased his appetite and after another massive meal he collapsed and died.

2. Roman Curses and the Mysterious Waters

Bath is the only place in England where a great deal of hot mineral water rises naturally from the ground. In fact there are at least three seperate hot springs that surface within a few hundred yards of each other in the centre of the city. One comes up at what is now the Cross Bath. Another is just around the corner at the Hot Bath. The third, and by far the largest, rises at the King's Bath; at least $\frac{1}{4}$ million gallons of mineral water come up daily. The Romans were the first to control this supply as they built a watertight container around the spring to act as a reservoir from which they could fill their complex of baths. No-one has ever used the waters as the Romans did. Apart from its obvious uses – the

Romans loved bathing – they also saw the springs as a form of wishing well. The mysterious, steaming waters, welling up from a great distance below the earth, had magical properties. Through them the Romans could get in touch with the gods. Offerings to them were thrown into the waters: although there were often strings attached. The gods might be asked to help the giver or, at least, to hinder his adversary. One inscription combines curse, plea and amateur detective work. Written backwards (so that only the gods could understand it) the inscription reads:

'May he who carried off Villia from me become as liquid as the water, May she who so obscenely devoured her become dumb, whether VELVINNA, EXSUPEREUS, SEVERINUS, AUGUSTALIS, COMITIANUS, CATUSMINIANUS, GERMANILLA or JOVINA'.

This is an interesting list as some of the girl's potential abductors are male, but others are female. Another curse offers a bribe. The goddess is promised the donor's cloak if she causes the death of Maximus who stole it in the first place.

One find is particularly intriguing. A barbed bronze fish hook was discovered in the water. Perhaps it was a peculiar type of offering; or perhaps even in those days there were those who crept back in the evening and tried to hook out the more valuable objects dropped in by the pious.

Death-dealing curses were restricted to the Roman period but occasionally the waters have produced odd phenomona to further emphasise the fact that they are something special. For centuries no-one was quite sure why the water was hot. Some said it was chemical decomposition far beneath the earth. Others claimed that volcanic activity must be responsible. On more than one occasion some nervous inhabitants have left the city after rumours went around that there was about to be an eruption and that Beechen Cliff was in imminent danger of sliding down into the city. It was many years before it was realised the waters are hot for the simple reason that the nether reaches from which they arise are naturally hot.

Roman head, Roman Baths Museum

Nevertheless, it is harder to explain other happenings. Once the main spring vomited up nuts, some rotten and black but others quite fresh. In the 17th Century occured a memorable incident when the King's Bath seemed to explode. James I's wife, Anne of Denmark, was just about to step into the waters when a flame shot up from the bottom of the cistern. Understandably upset, the Queen steadfastly refused to use the bath and went off to another, henceforth known as the Queen's Bath. This clearly did not worry the locals who continued to use the King's Bath, flashes of blue flame notwithstanding.

"Bladud . . . dived into the mud"

3. The Prince and the Pigs

The traditional story of Bladud, the founder of Bath, is such an amalgam of different tales and elaborations that it is quite disappointing to turn to one of the earliest accounts, that of Geoffrey of Monmouth, and see how little is actually said. John Wood gives us one of the fullest accounts based, it must be said, on very flimsy evidence.

According to Wood, Bladud was the only son of Lud Hudibras, king of the Britons. While a young man, he contracted the disease leprosy, at which point the court, rather unfairly, petitioned the king to get rid of him for fear of the disease spreading. Bladud was forced to leave.

He wandered for a short while until he fell in with a poor shepherd. The two talked about the weather, a popular topic even in 800 B.C., or so it appears. Bladud also picked up the idea that he ought to find a job and at Keynsham he took charge of a herd of pigs from a local swineherd.

The obvious happened. The pigs caught the prince's leprosy and in a desperate attempt to prevent the swineherd from realising what had happened, Bladud proposed to take the pigs over the river to seek the acorns in the forest there. The swineherd agreed, but realising that he had only bought himself a little more time, Bladud was still very depressed. The next morning, according to plan, he led the pigs over the river. The weather was good and Bladud stopped to pray for some answer to his problems. He did not receive quite the answer he was hoping for. As he communed with the gods, the pigs ran off down the valley and towards the warm, boggy mass in which the hot springs of Bath boiled up. In they jumped and so happy were they that Bladud could not get them out of the mud for many hours. At last they became hungry and a trail of acorns was laid to entice them to higher ground.

So far things had not gone at all well. As an apprentice swineherd Bladud had seen his herd become infected, run away from him and then ignore him by wallowing all day in

11

the mud. Undaunted, the prince now tried to put into effect a desperate plan. He would separate each pig in the hope that this would stop the spread of the infection; and he would keep them as clean as possible in the hope that their leprosy would clear up.

Already that first evening he seemed to have had some success. As he washed the mud off them, some pigs seemed to have started to get better. Bladud thought that this must be because of his 'clean and separate' tactics: as yet he had no inkling of the power of the muddy waters of Bath.

Luckily, one of his best sows then disappeared and was missing for seven days. At last Bladud found her wallowing in the mud and discovered that the week-long immersion had cleared her of all infection. Realising at last what was going on, Bladud stripped naked and dived into the mud. A few days of this treatment and he was completely cured as well. Wasting no time, he drove the now completely cured pigs back to their owner, revealed his identity and returned to the court. Later in gratitude Bladud both rewarded the swineherd handsomely and built the city of Bath where the leprosy curing waters bubbled out of the earth.

Bath has, throughout history, displayed some pride in the legend of Bladud and the pigs. After all, relatively few cities can claim to trace their foundation back to one particular event in the far distant past and the story of Bladud is an excellent advert for the city in its combination of royalty and the healing powers of the waters. It is all the more annoying, therefore, to some locals that the story of their princely founder has not always been taken as seriously as some would like.

Some would put this down to local jealousy. For a start, there was one slight embarrasment in the original story: after all, it was the pigs that first discovered the peculiar properties of the water. A number of late medieval writers from neighbouring towns and cities were soon suggesting that Bladud may have gone but that the pigs still remained in the guise of the local inhabitants. They gave as good as they got, though, as in an old poem with the immortal lines:

'The hogs thus banished by the prince,
Have lived in Bristol ever since'

Local historians have also tended to emphasise just the part
of Bladud's history concerning Bath. Admittedly there are
many different versions but the earliest of these did include a
second story that did not show up the prince in such a good
light. Having been cured of his skin disease, Bladud returned to his father's court and eventually became King. He
then seems to have become a little overambitious. He
decided he wanted to fly. Having made a pair of wings he
climbed onto the roof of the temple to Apollo, jumped off
and went straight down: 'his body being broken into many
pieces' as one medieval writer puts it. That the founder of
Bath came to a rather messy end due entirely to his own folly
is a tale usually left out in most stories of Bladud.

Nevertheless, the local authorities were rightly proud of
their royal founder. By the 16th Century there was a thriving
cottage industry built on the Bladud legend although he
never quite made it to national prominence. He only just
missed it though: Shakespeare wrote one of his greatest plays
about Bladud's son, King Lear, but without mentioning the
father. In the 17th Century the corporation took the Bladud
legend even further. They put up a statue of him at the baths
and the walls there had fulsome inscriptions to him. Even
so, not every visitor to the city accepted the story of Bladud,
as put forward by the council: the inscriptions were a little
too exaggerated for some of them to stomach. The noted wit
and friend of Charles II, the Earl of Rochester, was one who
became sick of the emphasis on Bladud on a visit to Bath.
Unfortunately for the local authorities, Rochester could do
better than merely grumble to his friends. He composed a
wicked poem casting severe doubts on the veracity of the
legend. The corporation said nothing but the inscriptions
were taken down.

The legend survived this temporary set-back. In the 18th
Century the architect John Wood wrote with great enthusiasm, but doubtful accuracy, a long account of Bladud's
history adding all the little details that people wanted to

"Passenger comfort was rarely considered"

know. When he built the Circus he commemorated the story by topping the houses with giant acorns, the pigs' favourite food. The corporation named one of their first housing developments Bladud's Buildings. The statue of Bladud still stands at the King's Bath: after all, whatever the truth of Bladud and the pigs, it does remain a good story.

4. What a Carry-on

Many 18th Century prints of Bath show the popular form of transport of the time: the sedan chair. This device was of great use to the well-dressed dandy and those who took the waters, for even at the time of its greatest popularity the city's streets left a great deal to be desired. Many were unpaved, covered with refuse and extremely muddy in wet weather. Few were lit at night. The sedan chair was the essential form of transport for those who could afford it. Many Georgian houses even had especially wide staircases and landings so that the chair could be brought right up to your room. The traveller sat back and the chairmen took the strain; and a fair strain it was, at times, on the hills of Bath.

Yet before one feels too much sympathy for the chairmen, gamely carrying their overweight gout-ridden passengers up hill after hill, it must be said that these men took full advantage of their monopoly of local transport; and despite the orderly impression given in the contemporary prints it is hard to find any writer who had a good word to say for them. Passenger comfort was rarely considered. Smollett complained that most men left their chairs outdoors all night so that the 'almost perpetual rain' turned them into boxes of wet leather. The inner lining became saturated with rain water, guaranteed to give a chill to those still sweating after immersion in the hot mineral waters.

The state of the chair was only the first problem: then came the tricky question of payment. Fares were supposed to depend on distance and number of hills. Taking a stranger to Bath by the long route from lodgings to baths might bring in more money but was also physically tiring so chairmen hit on a far easier way to increase profits: take the customer by the quickest route but then refuse to let him out of the chair until he had paid as much as was demanded. Stubborn fares would literally be trapped in their chairs. As an added encouragement, if it was raining, the top of the sedan chair would be left open to the discomfort of the traveller.

Even if you wished, it was difficult to avoid the attentions of the chairmen who were often a little too keen for business. As balls always ended at a set time, the people leaving the Assembly Rooms would be besieged by a scrummage of chairmen, all shouting for custom and fighting amongst themselves. The place soon became one sprawling mass: one reason for the decline of the lower Assembly Rooms was the fact that there was not enough room for many chairs and traffic jams invariably developed. Beau Nash tried to solve the problem by telling people to book sedan chairs in advance but the chairmen continued to be too keen. On one occasion a small group of nobles had stayed on at the lower rooms after the ball had finished. Accordingly, a number of chairmen had also waited around, hoping for a number of rich customers. But the night was clear and warm and when the nobles finally decided to go home, they ignored the chairmen and set off walking. The chairmen, having waited for some hours, were somewhat upset. The nobles were walking through the Abbey Churchyard when they were hit by dirt and rubbish thrown by persons unknown. It would not be hard to hazard a guess at the culprits.

Not that the chairmen had it all their own way. One noble was seen caning his men on the Grand Parade because they were so drunk they could not even hold the chair up. Chairmen who were rude or insolent often provoked gentlemen into drawing their swords on them. The ladies would take fright but the chairmen would retaliate and defend themselves with their chair poles. Many public assemblies ended in such confusion; indeed, one of the main reasons that Nash wanted to prevent swords being worn was not because of gentlemanly duels but because of their frequent clashes with the chairmen.

Nash introduced a number of improvements to tidy up the situation. Chairs had to be licensed. Conditions were laid down fixing charges and chairmen could be fined 10 shillings (50p) if they tried to charge more, refused to carry a customer or used abusive language or behaviour. The sedan chair continued, therefore, as a favoured form of transport until the paved roads of the 19th Century led to the introduction of the much less exciting Bath chair.

5. John Wood and the Corrupt Councillors

One fact that soon becomes evident to any visitor with only a few hours to spend in Bath is that the city's most famous architect didn't build that much in the centre of the city. The great public buildings and the streets within the confines of the old medieval limits were mostly designed by lesser names while Wood had to hunt around for private commissions often on land thought unsuitable for building and not owned by the council; for it was the council which played the main part in deciding who did, and who did not, get the plum commissions for redeveloping Bath and Wood's name seems to have rarely appeared on their short list.

It must be admitted that many of Wood's original ideas were somewhat bizarre. He was an outsider with some strange ideas on the history of Bath which he elaborated in a number of books. He talked at great length about the local druids and their local university; and spoke vaguely of human sacrifices on top of the nearby hill of Little Solsbury. His evidence was, to say the least, a little suspect. Bubbling with enthusiasm he also wrote in minute detail of the Romans in Bath at a time when very little was known about them. Undaunted, Wood announced he would turn Bath into a modern Rome. He planned big: amongst his projects were a Grand Circus for exhibitions of sports, an Imperial Gymnasium for the practice of medicinal exercises and a Royal Forum as a grand place of assembly. As none of these was ever completed the exact nature of these edifices remains obscure. The council declared them 'chimerical': weird would be one way of putting it: and rejected them out of hand.

However, the council continued to maintain a lack of interest even in Wood's less ambitious and far more sensible plans. Their reasons were not always strictly honourable. By the time Wood arrived in Bath the city was already extremely popular. There was not only a pressing need for accomodation but also most of the public buildings were fast becoming full to capacity. Yet little was done. The council owned most of the land and lodging houses inside the old city walls and they saw it as in their best interest to prevent new buildings so as to keep accomodation scarce and rents high. Much of the land outside the walls was held by the council in trust for the freemen of the city; and as the profits from this land were divided equally amongst freemen and councillors there was, again, little incentive to build. A more questionable practice was that the city architect decided who should be awarded particular building commissions; but the best ones he would often keep for himself. Wood never became city architect and therefore had the misfortune to see his plans regularly dismissed.

He certainly did not give up on the first attempt. He worked out a plan to redevelop the entire baths complex. The council turned him down. He narrowed his attention to the Pump Room which did seem a safe bet: although it was less than 40 years old it was already far too small to cater for all those who wanted to take the waters. It was too hot in summer, too cold in winter and had an unfashionable stone

18

South Parade

floor. Even the council knew it was too small; but the over-flow of visitors were going to Shaylors, a nearby coffee house, which was run by the mayor's son so to prevent the loss of trade the mayor blocked Wood's plan.

According to Wood, Bath also lost the chance for him to build a new Theatre, a General Hospital, a Grammar School . . . the list appears endless. At last, though, Wood was given a chance to develop an area near the centre over-looking what is now the Parade Gardens. Backed up by Nash, Wood was given the commission. The council were not being too helpful though: the area was very low-lying and flooded regularly owing to its proximity to the river: 'little better than an unfathomable bog' as one person described it. Wood confounded his critics though by buil-ding up the whole area on massive foundations and using designs left over (because they were deemed too expensive) from his work on Queen Square. But, according to Wood, the council had the last laugh. Having successfully com-pleted this area, North and South Parade, Wood then saw the council alter the charges for sedan chairs so that it became more expensive to take travellers east from the city centre, towards the Parade, than to take them anywhere else. It is no surprise, then to discover that most of Wood's greatest achievements were outside the centre and for private speculators. They, at least, played fair.

The council realised fairly late on that building developments could make profits for them, hence the lack of great Georgian architecture in the very centre of the city. Along the way they not only turned down Wood but also the great interior designer Robert Adam (his plans for an assembly room were too expensive) and the famous engineer Thomas Telford (ditto for his plans for a new Bath bridge). When areas were developed it often meant the council giving permission to a councillor, a rather ques-tionable practice. Trim Street was developed by Mr.Trim, a councillor. Daniel Milsom, another councillor, developed Milsom Street under an agreement by which the whole area eventually reverted to the council. Nor was it averse to making arrangements with other individuals. William Pulteney needed land for an approach road to his proposed bridge. The council gave him the necessary land in return for some land of his own on the other side of the river where the council could put up their new prison.

Nepotism was clearly never a problem that worried the council. In particular the City Architect seemed to have had not only the prerogative on vetoing architect's plans but also of giving the best commissions to himself. Thomas Attwood was one city architect who took full advantage of his position. He leased land from the council on which he built Bladud's Buildings, Oxford Row and part of the Paragon. He put up two houses so close to the Abbey that he blocked out the light there. He stopped Wood's plans for redeveloping the baths; but he saved his main energy for the battle over the proposal for a new Guildhall. Over a thirteen year span Attwood managed to block the plans of five different architects until eventually he had his own plan accepted. Unfortunately, one of his rivals, Palmer, had produced an equally good plan and one which even Attwood admitted was cheaper. An acrimonious argument developed which came to a melodramatic conclusion. Attwood, while surveying an old house in the market place, fell through the floor and died of severe head wounds.

Even then Palmer did not take over. Baldwin became city architect, pulled down Attwood's half-built walls and put up a Guildhall to his own design. Baldwin built for the council Beau, Union and Bath streets but then became so wrapped up in the private development of the Bathwick estate that he neglected his council job. After a series of warnings he was fired by the council. Unfortunately he had just started building a new Pump Room. This time Palmer did get to finish the task.

The Obelisk, Queen Square constructed to commemorate a royal visit that never took place

6. The Vicar and the Prostitutes

Although Bath has long been known for its amusements, the less salubrious of these have rarely merited a mention. Yet at one time to call someone a 'woman of Bath' was tantamount to calling her a prostitute.

The lack of information on this topic is partly explained by the fact that the great local historians of the 19th Century tended to be clergymen and they preferred to draw a discreet veil over the more dubious aspects of the past. The one great exception was the Reverend W.J. Bolton who not only waged increasing war on one pocket of prostitution in the city but also wrote a booklet about his struggle.

In all fairness, it would have been hard for Reverend Bolton to totally ignore the seamier side of Bath. He was the vicar of St. James, a rather splendid Georgian church that stood where Woolworth stands today. Diagonally opposite, and barely a hundred yards away, was the cramped St. James Court, some twenty houses inhabited, according to Bolton, by some sixty prostitutes. Bolton not only objected to their profession but also to the facts that they were frequently drunk, got into fights and encouraged the playing of the piano at all hours. Even on Sunday the women touted for custom: one has visions of Bolton's congregation leaving church and being confronted by these ladies: and so the good vicar launched a full-scale crusade against this den of iniquity.

His first hope was that the police would do something but they said they could not help. He asked the corporation to buy up the whole court, knock it down and put up respectable housing. They did nothing. Bolton referred in his account to certain influential people actively opposing him being too interested themselves in breaking the 7th Commandment (Thou shalt not commit adultery) but, unfortunately for posterity, he was too cautious to name names. Undaunted, he decided to take action on his own. His first attempt was a little optimistic: he approached brothel keepers and quoted extracts from the Bible at them. He had more success when he threatened to bring prosecutions against them. Some gave up their trade immediately. Others fled the city.

Bolton had a great enthusiasm for getting the Court's inhabitants away from its pernicious influences. He fixed up posts for penitent prostitutes to become servants at various seaside resorts (although a number soon crept back to Bath). He walked into one brothel only to find a woman there stark naked. This may not seem to us to be that much of a surprise but Bolton accepted her explanation that her clothes had been taken away to prevent her leaving the building. He brought her new outfits and found her another job.

He tried new ideas with the brothel-keepers. He encouraged them to send their children off to be educated elsewhere, after frequently having to baptise them first and marry their parents. But his greatest success was in appealing to their greed. Bolton set up a trust to buy out brothel-keepers and turn their houses over to more whole-some purposes. This was so successful that in the final pages of his booklet Bolton announced he would now begin to buy up and clean up other areas of vice in the city. Alas for posterity once again. He remained coy as to where such places were. St. James Court no longer exists but one cannot help wondering where S—— Place and T—— Street, Bolton's next two targets, were and whether they exist today.

7. The Firing of the Chapel

Bath has never had much of a reputation for rioting; but at times a certain element within the city has felt the urge to join in with national disturbances, with varying results. The greatest disturbance came in 1780 when in London the Gordon riots caused widespread destruction as various groups of bigots protested against giving Catholics a better deal. Now this should not have affected Bath; the city had rarely taken religion that seriously nor had the Catholics done anything to annoy anyone as they had kept an extremely low profile for well over two hundred years. Unfortunately, and with impeccably bad timing, this was about to change. No-one could have predicted the London riots but just as they were starting the Catholics had finally completed their first purpose-built chapel in Bath since the Reformation. It stood in St. James Parade, near to the house of the local Catholic leader, Dr. Brewer, and was due to open on Sunday June 11.

So just when the Catholics were being attacked in London, the local congregation in Bath found itself attracting unwanted attention as well. Things began to stir on the Friday, June 9, and by the end of the day a host of different groups seemed to be heading for the chapel and for a variety of motives. First of all, a small mob began to gather and walk through the city crying 'No Popery' while making for the chapel. Next a small party of the local militia, the Volunteers, were sent by the corporation to guard the building. The commander read the riot act but the crowd stayed so the Volunteers stayed as well. Then at midnight a reinforcement group of Volunteers turned up, at which point everything went wrong. This second group was led by a Captain Dupervé who had the bright idea of ordering his men not to load their muskets. But as a form of protection he had the less bright idea of telling them to fix bayonets. This did not please the mob. As Dupervés' men elbowed their way through the crowd, chunks of wood and firebrands came hurtling towards them. A shot rang out. One of the mob fell dead. The rest went berserk. The Volunteers took one look, turned tail, and fled. At last the mob were able to get into the chapel and indulge in typical mob activities. Both the chapel and Dr. Brewer's house were looted and set on fire. The contents were dragged out into the streets to form the basis of large bonfires. For good measure a further four houses were put to the torch as well.

Dr. Brewer, luckily, was not at home at the time. Sensing the atmosphere he had been one of the few people actually heading away from the chapel that Friday. He had then spent a few hours reliving the parable of the Good Samaritan. One tavern after another refused to take him in and help him. He turned in desperation to the Guildhall but the corporation refused to even open the door to him. At last the White Hart took pity on him and took him in. Brewer managed to slip out the back of the pub and over the river to safety.

By the time the troops had arrived from other towns the riot was over and all they could do was to damp the fires. The chapel had already burnt itself out and the mob had dispersed. The corporation, at last, sprang into action and attempted to do the decent thing but no-one admitted to firing the fatal shot and no-one was ever accused. One man by the name of Butler was put on trial for organising the riot. Found guilty, he was hanged before a large and appreciative crowd although perhaps it was in rather bad taste to execute him at the site of his 'triumph', St. James Parade. A large contingent of troops was in Bath to guard against a last minute rescue attempt but none was made. Butler went to the gallows protesting his innocence and claiming that he had been framed.

There was one final act. Dr. Brewer, still smarting over his treatment by the corporation, put in a claim for generous compensation and, for once, the corporation did pay up.

8. Well, Well

It is no exaggeration to say that Bath's fame has long rested on its hot spa waters. Many, many people have come to the city to seek a cure; and amongst them have always been those who have hoped to discover a new hot spring themselves and make a fortune.

The waters were much coveted by the corporation which had been granted the right to look after them in the reign of Elizabeth I. The corporation was always very conscious of the fact that a number of baths might be fed by only one spring: so the more water one bath got, the less the others did. John Wood tells the tale of one chance discovery. Workmen were building houses on the site of Abbey House. One of them raised a flagstone on the floor of one room and immediately water gushed up from the ground; apparently the flagstone had been acting as some sort of plug. The delighted tenant of the house promptly decided to set up his own baths on the site. The jealous corporation objected, claiming that this was impossible as the water came from the municipally owned King's spring. This proved untrue and the objections were dropped.

The hope that you might find a spring under your property and, in doing so, make a fortune led many to go prospecting. Few struck lucky. One who did was a William Skrine who owned land to one side of the Hot Bath. His digging produced a spring which the corporation, once again, claimed was part of their property. Once again, their protest failed. Inspired by this, William Swallow began digging in the cellar of his house. Down and down he went until he ran into a buried mill-stone. This proved too great an obstacle and the dig ended somewhat abruptly.

The next best thing to a hot spring was a cold water spring but few lasted long or achieved much fame. Few had such a swift blaze of publicity as the Lyncombe House Spa. Here, in 1737, a Dr. Milsom had rented a fishpond. Investigating a leak he began crawling into the tangled undergrowth where he discovered a strange sight: a patch of ground that looked like a glutinous pile of frogspawn, that smelt of sulphur and was shaking. Dr. Milsom began to dig at this spot and discovered a spring that was the colour of whitewash. A few simple experiments seemed to have convinced him that this was indeed a new source of mineral water. The doctor then hit on a particularly novel way of getting publicity for his find. He invited all the chief tradesmen of Bath to a party and in front of them all he added his mineral water to brandy. The mixture turned purple and black. This clearly showed that this water was different but unfortunately it was so unusual that the guests refused to drink it. Dr. Milsom suddenly found himself with a large quantity of unwanted, purple, brandy. He refused to let it go to waste, though, and after the guests had been drinking for a while their inhibitions were loosened. The doctor then explained about his mineral water and everyone downed the brandy as well. Dr. Milsom had got all the publicity he could want.

But now he faced a dispute with another doctor who put forward a claim to ownership of the spring. The quarrel dragged on without result but in the meantime it was agreed to put up an impressive building over the spring to attract further attention. Alas for all concerned: the foundations went down so far that they disturbed the spring and it dried up. No-one made any money out of it after all.

The most famous cold spa was that at the bottom of Beechen Cliff, developed by Mr. Greenaway in the early 18th Century. A spring supplied a bath that attracted a fair amount of attention in its day, although few probably believed the argument that it was in fact a hot spring that turned suddenly cold when it issued from the ground because the bottom of Beechen Cliff was always in shadow. It only lost popularity in the late 19th Century and the bath house itself survived well into the present century, although the bath had long been floored over.

Other springs had shorter life spans. Winifreds Well, on Lansdown, produced a mineral water that was taken with sugar. Bathford Spa was another spring discovered by acci-

"The flagstone had been acting as
some sort of plug"

dent when a miller by the name of Arnold Townsend was cutting down the trees in part of a field he had just bought. In the centre of a cleared area ran a spring which discoloured everything it touched. Encouraged by a neighbour, Townsend sent off some of the water for analysis and it proved to have traces of minerals. It soon became used by those with wounds and running sores, but Townsend had no real interest in the business and sold it to a doctor.

Perhaps because Bath was such a centre for medicine, any mineral spring could attract a specialised clientele. Carn-well on Lansdown was reputedly good for disorders of the eye. Lime Kiln Spa, also on Lansdown, was praised for the treatment of diabetes. A carpenter by the name of James Hellier had been suffering from this complaint but could not afford to travel to Bristol to take the softer and more expensive waters there. The spring that rose near a Lime Kiln on Lansdown was much closer so he took the waters and seemed to be cured. This was good news for John Hobbs, a Bristol merchant who owned the land, and he built a cistern, buildings where one could drink the waters, and a bathhouse. This attracted the envy of a neighbour, Sir Phillip Parker Long, who owned land lower down the hill and by various devices managed to draw off some of the spring water to his property where he also began to put up buildings where one could take the waters.

As at Lyncombe Spa, greed met its just reward: the spring ceased to run. Many, many cold springs have appeared around Bath but they have never been as consistent nor as popular, as the ever-constant hot waters that have made the city so famous.

9. "Ease, Disease, . . . Lechery and Sport"

As a spa town, Bath has rarely had a shortage of medical practitioners. Indeed, there were so many there in the 18th Century that one wit suggested that they should be rationed to two per patient. When a visitor arrived in Bath he could be mobbed by the agents of various landlords, all eager to whisk him off to their particular lodging house where they could fix him up with a doctor, a physician and an apothecary. Each house would also claim that the nearest bath was by far the best for his particular complaint.

The doctors themselves were a mixed bunch including some notable eccentrics. Dr. Seneschall practiced alchemy, trying to turn base metals into gold, and was known to walk around in the height of summer dressed in a heavy fur coat. All doctors in Bath were famous for their ability to make money: none came cheap and few patients got the better of them. One very rich gentleman came to Bath to take the waters in the hope that they would immediately clear up his gout. The cure did not have such a rapid effect however but the gentleman disliked the idea of parting with his money in order to consult with a doctor. He hit on a good idea. While walking in the street he hailed a medical friend that he happened to meet. Having told him of his problem, the gentleman asked his friend what he should take. 'Advice' retorted the doctor who then walked off.

Beau Nash was one of the few to cross swords with a member of the medical profession and come out on top. Complaining of various pains, he called in a doctor who wrote some instructions on a piece of paper, told Nash to follow them and said he would return the following day. This was a favourite tactic of those doctors who were paid for each visit and realising that he was being taken for a ride, Nash decided to retaliate. When the doctor returned the next day he asked whether Nash had followed his advice. No, replied the patient, for if he had followed his advice he would have broken his neck. This naturally left the doctor nonplussed until Nash went on to explain what he meant: as soon as the doctor had left the previous day, Nash had screwed the prescription up and thrown it out of the window, taking care not to follow it – at least in the literal sense. The doctor retired discomforted; Nash made a speedy recovery to full health.

The inhabitants of Bath had a certain disregard for the medical staff. In part this may have been a form of jealousy: for many years the main hospitals of the city were only open to visitors. Locals could not be admitted. The Mineral Water Hospital charged £3 caution money when a patient was admitted which covered the cost of the burial if things went wrong. Rumours of death and burial surrounded the hospital. It was claimed that it was built close to the city walls so that if a patient did die, the hospital could save the expense of a funeral by taking the body by night and throwing it over the walls and, hence, outside the city's jurisdiction. This surely must be an exaggeration.

It was noted that few doctors practiced what they preached. As the writer Anstey commented:

'Since the day that King Bladud first found out the bogs,
And thought them so good for himself and his hogs,
Not one of the Faculty ever has tried,
These exalted waters to cure his own hide!'

But it was also noted that few of the cures: pills, potions, prescriptions: had that much effect anyway. The most renowned doctor in Bath was Doctor Oliver creator of the Oliver biscuit which had no miracle ingredient but was just full of plain ingredients that gave your stomach a rest from rich food. Perhaps even more important was the fact that, as sharp observers noted, few visitors to Bath seemed to require urgent medical attention. By the 18th Century it had long been realised that illness tended to get in the way of the main pursuit in Bath, pleasure. You might say that you were going to the spa to take the cure, but you would not enjoy the city if you were actually ill. As Charles II's friend, Rochester, summed up the attractions of Bath:

'Ten thousand Pilgrims thither do resort
For ease, disease, for lechery and sport'.

10. The Grey Lady of the Theatre Royal

Bath's Theatre Royal can lay claim to being the centre of one of the most haunted areas in the city. Around the corner, in what is now a restaurant, resides the ghost of Beau Nash's mistress Juliana Popjoy who has frightened away at least one potential customer. In the public house next door, The Garrick's Head, there have been a whole host of unexplained phenomena from poltergeist activities such as flying candlesticks to strange noises, smells and sights.

In the theatre a clock struck three times during a performance in 1963 which was a little strange considering the mechanism had been removed beforehand and the hands stood at 12.30. There is also the small matter of a tortoiseshell butterfly that has materialised at pantomime time each and almost every year since 1948 when a pantomime in that year featured a butterfly ballet.

But the most famous ghost connected with the theatre is that of the grey lady. She appears, irregularly, in an upper circle box inside the theatre dressed in an evening gown with a feather in her hair, gloves on her hands and an aroma of jasmine around her. She is sometimes fullbodied, at other times a little hazy, but always completely grey. In 1963 a dancer was rehearsing a new song when he became conscious that he was being watched. Knowing nothing of the legend, he looked up to the circle where he saw the faint outline of a woman.

In 1978 she was in far more substantial a form. Two girls

"She appears, irregularly, in an
upper circle box"

sitting in the upper circle not only saw the grey lady sitting near them but also saw her actually turn and wave at them. So frequent have been the sightings that some casts see it as lucky for her to appear during the run of their play. In 1981 a number of students from the drama department of Bath Technical College mounted a sponsored event with a difference: they maintained a week-long vigil, both night and day, from the opposite box in an attempt to spot the grey lady but she did not appear. She has been seen elsewhere in the theatre, on staircases, corridors and even in the reflection in the mirror of a dressing room but who she is: or rather was: remains a mystery.

There are many explanations as to her origin. One says that she was an 18th Century woman who threw herself from a window when her lover was killed. Either she had two lovers who fought a duel in which her particular favourite was killed; or worse still, she was married and the lover was killed by her husband. Alternatively, she was an actress who fell in love with a gentleman who was a regular visitor to the theatre and who always sat in an upper circle box. Sadly, her love was not returned and in despair the girl hanged herself from a door in the Garrick's Head next door. This seems rather similar to the death of 'Sylvia' in John Wood's house in Queen Square but perhaps it was a popular means of suicide at the time. In fact one visitor to the Garrick's Head complained of a choking feeling while she slept and in the morning discovered red marks around her neck, as if she had had a rope around it.

A few years ago further details did emerge about the ghost. Her name appeared to be Delia and she had been unhappy in love. She had died suddenly, and possibly by her own hand, at the age of 27 in the year 1812. Such details would seem conclusive except that they were produced at a seance held by the local ghost chronicler Margaret Royal and the cast of the play 'Blithe Spirit'. Historical information based only on one source is always suspect and unfortunately seances are yet to be accepted by most historians as legitimate source material. However the ghost intimated that her story could be verified properly by the fact that her name

could be found on a playbill on the wall of the so-called
Green Room in the theatre. Unfortunately the entire theatre
was gutted by fire in 1862 and in the rebuilding it was exten-
sively remodelled; few traces of the original interior remain.
The grey lady seems not to have been put off by the drastic
alterations to the theatre that she seems to know so well.

John Wood's house, Queen Square

11. The Tragic Suicide of Sylvia

Wood tells the tragic story of 'Sylvia', a girl who suffered all forms of degradation until she finally decided to end it all. Many guesses have been made as to her real identity yet the truth is almost unnecessary. It is a tale that all too vividly shows the darker side, and the sorrow, behind the gambling and glittering parties of 18th Century Bath.

By all accounts, Sylvia was one of those girls who began with every possible advantage in life. She was beautiful, witty and rich. People in large numbers flocked to be with her; but in this lay her ruin. Her appearance at an event would guarantee its success and she fell in with unscrupulous people who used her for their own selfish purposes, to attract others to their assemblies. Sylvia became attracted and then addicted to the gambling tables. Gossip began to develop: she was accused of being of easy virtue. Meanwhile she slid further and further into debt.

In 1730 Sylvia became a lodger in Wood's house in Queen Square. Wood could find nothing but praise for her, but already the damage had been done. Secretly she was consulting with doctors as to the easiest and least painful way of committing suicide. Yet even in the house there were one or two signs of how disturbed she was. At night she found it hard to sleep and could be heard walking around and around her bedroom for hours on end in a vain attempt to bring exhaustion.

In 1731 tragedy occured. Wood was away in London on a commission and rather than just leave Sylvia in the house with his youngest children he got one of his most trusted workmen to sleep there for added security. Wood had promised to return on 8th September but the job took longer than planned and as evening approached on the appointed day it became clear that he would not return then. Sylvia looked more and more disappointed as the day wore on. As night fell she used a diamond to scratch a final message on the dining room window:

'O death! thou pleasing end to human woe,
Thou cure for life, thou greatest good below!
Still may'st thou fly the coward and slave,
And thy soft slumbers only bless the brave.'

She owed great sums of money, she had run out of friends
prepared to lend her more and now she took the decision to
kill herself. This appeared to take a load off her mind. For
the rest of the evening she played happily with Wood's children and then retired to bed at her usual hour having first
wished her servant a good night. This was the first time she
had ever done so.

Her subsequent actions are largely conjecture. She
retired to bed but soon got up again. She dressed all in
white, in her best clothes as if she were a bride. She took
some silk and some gold lengths of cord to make a rope with
a noose. Then she took a few books. One that was later
found open concerned the story of a girl who was ruined by
the treachery and ingratitude of her best friend: a message
for those who found her body perhaps?

Sylvia now made her final preparations. She put the
noose over her neck, got on a stool, opened a cupboard door
and looped the cord over the back of the door and locked it
shut. Then she jumped off the stool but the silk cord broke
and she fell heavily to the ground, bruising her forehead in
the process. The thump woke the workman in his bedroom.
He checked the time: it was 2.30 a.m. As Sylvia often walked
about at night, he thought no more about it and fell asleep
again.

Sylvia tried once more. She made a new noose out of a
stronger thread. This time she made no mistakes. She kicked
away the stool, the cord held but there was no instant snap
of the neck. It must have taken several minutes for her to
choke to death. In her death throes she bit through her tongue time and again.

Morning came. The servant, Nash, waited for her mistress to ring her bell at 7.00 a.m. as usual. She waited in
vain. After a while Nash tried the door but it was locked.
Eventually at 2.30 p.m. in the afternoon a workman put a

ladder up to the window. He lifted the sash, pushed the shutters back and saw an object in the furthest corner of the room that made him recoil in horror. He was persuaded to return, enter the room and, at last, get the key to unlock the door and let everyone in.

Sylvia was buried next day, a judge deciding that lunacy had led to her death. A close friend paid for the funeral. Months later, her effects were auctioned off to pay her debts. They went for such high prices that all her creditors were paid off and a substantial profit made. The buyers claimed they wanted mementos of their great friend; as Wood remarks, it was a pity they were not prepared to pay out before she died in which case all this might have been avoided.

Her ghost is still said to haunt the house in Queen Square.

12. Swords of Honour

In a city full of gentlemen all too frequently exhibiting ungentlemanly behaviour, there was always the final resort of the duel. Officially frowned upon, the duel was the answer to accusations of cheating at cards, libel and slander, or any form of behaviour that merited some public apology or admittance of guilt. Most were fought with swords, although rarely to the death: honour was satisfied, once first blood had been drawn. Master of Ceremonies Captain Webster was one of the unlucky ones who was killed. Wounds could still prove tricky: one cheat at cards died nine years after a duel when an old wound opened up again.

Despite popular fiction, such encounters were not always displays of skilled swordsmanship. Many descended

Many of the stories in this book relate to specific locations. Start at the Roman Baths and follow the numbers on the map (which are the same as the numbers of the relevant stories in the text) for a pleasant walk round the sights of Bath – and their secrets!

1. A Cure for All Ills?
2. Roman Curses and the Mysterious Waters
3. The Prince and the Pigs
4. What a Carry-on
5. John Wood and the Corrupt Councillors
6. The Vicar and the Prostitutes
7. The Firing of the Chapel
8. Well, Well
9. "Ease, Disease, . . . Lechery and Sport"
10. The Grey Lady of the Theatre Royal
11. The Tragic Suicide of Syliva
12. Swords of Honour
13. A Victorian Murder
14. Behind the Façade
15. Riot at the Assembly Rooms
16. Jane Austen and the Case of the Planted Lace
17. "Attacking Satan at his Headquarters"
18. Squares in the Air

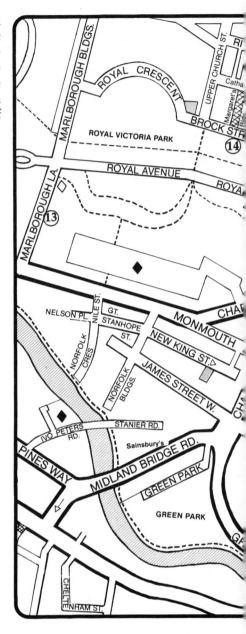

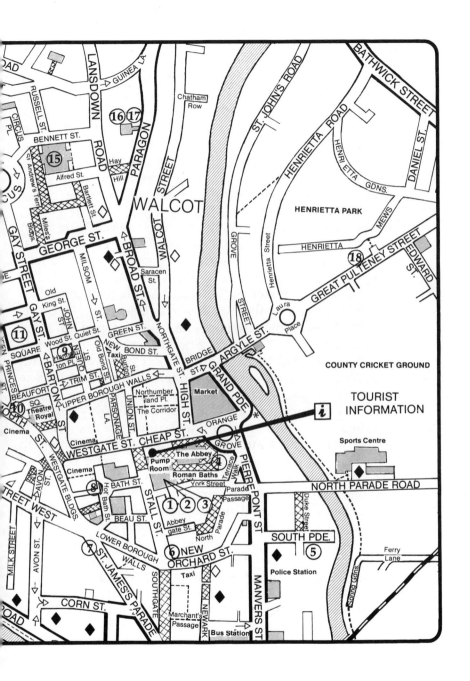

to levels of pure butchery. One such was fought by Richard Brinsley Sheridan. This famous writer and politician led an eventful life, having eloped with the famous beauty Elizabeth Ann Linley from her family home in the Royal Crescent. This greatly angered one of her unwanted suitors, a Major Matthews, who wrote a series of insulting letters to Sheridan. This goaded the latter into challenging Matthews to a duel which took place in London. Sheridan won, Matthews apologised but then started causing more trouble, leading to a second duel, this time at Kingsdown, near Bath.

Sheridan began by launching himself at Matthews in an attempt to snatch his sword away from him. He failed, but his attack and the uneven nature of the ground forced Sheridan to fall over, dragging his opponent down with him. The two swords were broken as they fell, and the men continued to grapple with each other in a hand to hand struggle. Eventually Matthews proved stronger and got on top of Sheridan calling on him to ask for mercy. Sheridan refused, but by this time Matthews had recovered the point of his sword with which he began to stab at his opponent in the neck and face and all over. Sheridan tried desperately to ward off the blows and this unequal, and far from gentlemanly, struggle continued for a number of minutes until the two seconds came to their senses and dragged Matthews off. Sheridan was taken away to the nearest tavern, in some pain: but public sympathy was with him. His wife rushed to his assistance and Matthews was never seen in Bath again.

Officialdom frowned upon duels and a too successful participant could find himself arrested on a charge of murder. Careful 'contestants' would try to avoid attracting attention. The Orange Grove by moon or torch light was one location. Another was the so-called 'Duelling Ground'; a depression in the ground at the town end of what is now Victoria Park, the theory apparently being that if you did kill your opponent, you were already on the outskirts of the city and could jump on your horse and be away before the local forces of law and order could get you.

Beau Nash had no great enthusiasm for duelling either,

The Duelling Ground

yet even he found himself involved in one. While at the baths one day, Nash was watching from the 'viewers gallery'. A gentleman beside him happened to make a number of compliments to one of the female bathers. Nash clearly felt this was unseemly behaviour but rather than cut him down to size with his ready tongue, he adopted a rather more physical approach and pushed the man over the rail into the water. Naturally, the gentleman was not happy, least of all because the lady he had praised happened to be his wife. He challenged Nash to a duel but it was a scrappy and half-hearted affair and Nash merely received a few scratches. The 'Beau' greatly exaggerated the story in the telling; and then banned duelling on the basis that having tried it himself he was now an expert in such matters.

Marlborough Buildings

13. A Victorian Murder

To be precise, the following story took place a number of years before Victoria ascended the throne but in its senselessness, violence and sudden dénouement, it has much in common with so many later tales avidly read by the 19th Century public. The murderer was both ruthless and clever; eventually too clever, as we shall see.

The killing took place in 1828 in a house in Marlborough Buildings, to the side of the Royal Crescent. Here lived an elderly spinster and her three servants: Richard Gilham, his wife and a maid by the name of Maria Bagnall. All the servants lived on the premises. It so happened that one day Gilham was walking by a room in the house when he overheard a conversation between Maria and her employer. Maria was making unfavourable comments about Gilham; so he decided to kill her.

A few unkind words rarely lead to murder but Gilham was clearly bent on revenge. Wasting no time, he decided to kill Maria that very night. He retired to bed early but stayed awake until midnight when he knew that Maria would still be downstairs but all alone. He turned to his wife, said that he was feeling ill and went down to the kitchen. Maria was not there. Then he heard a noise and realised she was performing some task outside. Gilham quietly crept behind the kitchen door to wait for her. As she walked back inside he sprang forward and attacked her with a wooden bludgeon, raining blows onto her until she fell to the ground. But Maria still fought back as hard as she could, screaming and struggling with her assailant. It was to no avail. In desperation Gilham drew a pen-knife and cut her throat, silencing her cries at last.

Possibly this act brought him back, at least in part, to his senses. A spur of the moment decision had led to a messy murder but now Gilham showed some ingenuity in trying to cover his tracks. First he washed the blood from his clothes. He returned to his bedroom, locked himself in and hid the key. Next, he took out a pistol, loaded it and fired it out of the window. Not surprisingly, the police rushed to the scene to be hailed by Gilham leaning out of the window, shouting that there were robbers in the house who had already locked him up. Suitably warned, the police moved in. While two watched the front of the building, others approached it from the rear only to find the kitchen door wide open and inside Maria's body on a floor awash with blood. Close study revealed footmarks in the back garden and marks on the rear wall. The solution was obvious: the thieves had escaped over the back wall after locking up Gilham and killing Maria.

Gilham seemed to be in the clear. His story fitted the facts (although why his employer and, more importantly his wife, seem to have said nothing is quite a mystery). The police questioned him carefully and his answers were detailed and well-considered. He was in the clear, he could relax; and here was his mistake. The police felt that considering all that had happened: robbery, imprisonment, the brutal murder of a colleague: Gilham was just a little too composed. Further enquiries were made and it was discovered that Gilham was renting an obscure lodging in Northampton Street. A search there revealed a number of items that he had stolen from his employer. Gilham was arrested.

While awaiting trial his nerve cracked and he at last confessed his guilt to the prison chaplain. But he then appeared to regain his composure and at the subsequent trial he claimed that this confession could not be submitted as evidence as it had been said in confidence to a clergyman. This appeal was rejected and it took only five minutes for the jury to decide he was guilty. Gilham was hanged soon after, his body being given to the Royal United Hospital to be dissected.

14. Behind the Façade

The buildings of Georgian Bath certainly look most impressive and quite substantial; but they were put up in a period when building regulations scarcely existed and if they do impress, then that was part of their purpose. Most Georgian builders trod a thin line between that which looked good, and that which was as cheap as possible.

To be strictly accurate, the famous architects: Wood, Adams, Baldwin and others: did not design complete houses. Most only drew up the front of the house. Impressive fronts hid narrow houses. Behind the magnificent façade was a different story altogether. Each houseowner would build as much as he could afford so although two fronts would be the same, the backs could vary tremendously in size depending on each owner's wealth: just take a look at the back of the Circus to see how messy such an approach could be. If you were not satisfied with living in an ordinary house, the designer could create the impression of something better. At a distance the north side of Queen Square looks like one, palatial whole: only a careful close up shows it to be a series of much smaller houses. Even the famed crescents were partly created to save money. The Royal Crescent follows a contour line around a shallow valley. If it was a straight line it would have needed massive foundations in the centre and for the ground to have been levelled. Queen Square was originally to have been built on flat ground as well, but architect John Wood could not afford to level it.

Wood built well. Many did not. Foundations were often inadequate. Many houses settled as in parts of Pulteney Street where once straight lines now dip and rise distinctly. Joists were used so sparingly that floors were said to sink with the tread of the foot. In Bath Street, opposite the Roman Baths, it was discovered a few years ago that the wooden supporting beams had rotted so far that the vertical front wall was unsupported and inclining towards the street. Small wonder that the common joke in the 18th Century was

"Ugly protuberances on the backs of
many of the better streets"

that when the 60 year leases fell in, so did the houses. A
survey before World War II revealed that many of Bath's
Georgian houses were so badly built that the fear was raised
that if a bomb landed at one end of Pulteney Street, the
whole lot would collapse like a pack of cards.

The idea of grandeur did not go far into the interior of
the house. In Nash's golden days, all entertaining was done
in the public buildings anyway. At home the high-ceilinged

rooms were notoriously hard to heat and the tinder and flint method of lighting fires could take half an hour to catch light. Bedrooms were so cold that many slept in curtained four poster beds. There was rarely any running water: servants had to carry supplies all the way to the top of the house. Their own quarters in the attics were notorious for being too cold in winter and too hot in summer.

But the main disadvantage was the lack of toilets. There were few indoors. The occasional 'specialised' bowl would be disguised as a piece of furniture. Sometimes pits were dug in the basement. Once they were full, the floor boards would be put back again and another hole dug elsewhere in the room. The best houses would have them regularly emptied by 'night men'. Outdoor toilets would often freeze over in the winter; but at many lodgings even this refinement did not exist. Georgian ladies usually announced they were going to 'pluck a rose' in the garden and out they would go behind the bushes. Wood did begin to install water closets in some of his buildings but they were not particularly successful. To put it bluntly, they smelt and most had to be stopped up. The need of later generations for the indoor toilet largely explains the ugly protuberances on the backs of many of the better streets in Bath: but the fronts still remain unsullied and as impressive as the Georgians intended.

15. Riot at the Assembly Rooms

The 'Master of Ceremonies' was a semi-official post intended to regulate and administer the various public gatherings that Bath became so famous for in the 18th Century. The title barely existed before that time for earlier visitors had to make their own entertainments in the evenings. With no pump room or assembly rooms, everyone had to cram into the extremely small Guildhall or put up their own marquee on what is now Orange Grove.

But even in the hey-day of Bath's popularity, the post 'Master of Ceremonies' seems to have regularly attracted the wrong sort of person. Captain Webster, at the start of the 18th Century, lacked most of the necessary attributes. A keen gambler, he was accused of cheating at cards and forced to agree to a duel. Unfortunately his skill at arms also left something to be desired and he was killed.

This left the post open to one of Webster's supporters, a relative newcomer to Bath, Richard 'Beau' Nash. Nash was the only man ever to make something of the title and in his own way he was perfectly suited to the job. As portraits show, he was certainly not called 'Beau' for his looks but he did dress well, live lavishly and tried to do everything with style. Like a wild west marshal, he cleaned up the town (literally: householders had to sweep their doorsteps regularly) and introduced a code of conduct to be observed at all public meetings and dances. A quick wit cut down potential troublemakers: when once it was suggested that he was immoral for having a mistress he replied 'A man can no more be termed a whoremonger for having one whore in his house, than a cheesemonger for having one cheese.' At times his wit was a little too sharp: on being told by a woman with a badly deformed back that she had come from London, he retorted that she had obviously not come 'straight' from there. In other ways he was not quite the perfect 'Master'. He was not a good gambler; the gambling houses appear to have given him money for attracting customers to their establishments. He was a poor writer and as he got older became something of a bore repeating, at great length, the more famous exploits of his youth. Gambling dens were closed down, Nash was left with little money until the council took pity and gave him a commission to write a book. They lavished even more money on his funeral, perhaps to make up for their ignoring him in the last years of his life.

Nash's successors fared even worse. Master of Ceremonies Derrick was a member of the upper classes who had fallen on hard times. Absolutely penniless, he slept most nights in the open streets and tried to make ends meet by writing particularly bad poems in honour of the more

The Assembly Rooms

important visitors. When Derrick vacated the post there were two rivals for the post, Brereton and Plomer. The genteel ladies of Bath split into two factions and brought out a rash of pamphlets in support of their candidate and opposing the other. So far, so good but then matters really began to get out of hand. A public meeting was held in the Assembly Rooms but tempers became heated and the meeting ended with Mr. Plomer being dragged out by his nose. A second gathering was held at the same venue but this time the ladies began fighting amongst themselves. Within a short time, the Assembly Rooms were a sea of heaving humanity as woman clawed at woman. The mayor was eventually called in but even he could only stop the fight by reading out the riot act.

Despite this interest, the calibre of the Masters does not seem to have improved. Our final candidate, in the mid 1770s, was a Captain Wade who, perhaps, did worst of all. He seduced the wife of a very important gentleman, was discovered, forced to pay damages and to resign his post. The 'Master of Ceremonies' continued, but with very little prestige!

Milsom Street at the time of Jane Austen

16. Jane Austen and the Case of the Planted Lace

'Bath was undoubtedly the dearest home of Jane Austen' according to one guidebook from early this century. Not so; the great author did make a number of visits to the city, lived there for a few years and set substantial portions of two of her novels: *Northanger Abbey* and *Persuasion*: in Bath; but she did not like it.

She was quite comprehensive in her dislike of the city. If first impressions are important, then hers were the worst. On her initial visit to Bath it never stopped raining and she felt thoroughly miserable. Then again, she hated it in good weather as well. Her second visit began on a sunny day but she complained that Bath was all vapour, shadow, smoke and confusion and that it looked better in the rain. When settled in Bath, she frequently complained of the dazzling 'white glare' of the local stone when the sun shone on it.

Her father decided to retire to Bath with his family in 1801; it was said that Jane fainted with unhappiness at the news. Few of her letters survive from the next three years when she lived in Bath, probably because they showed how unhappy she was and her sister Cassandra destroyed them as a result. She appears to have done little writing in Bath. She disliked at least one of her homes, in Green Park Buildings, because of the damps. And it was while at Bath that Jane received a number of items of bad news. The only man known to have made an offer of marriage to her died suddenly; and in 1804 her father passed away and was buried in Bath.

Many explanations have been given for Jane Austen's thorough dislike of the city: her love of the countryside, her distaste for a spa no longer fashionable and rapidly declining into empty ceremony: but there was also one particular incident which must have had some effect on her.

On her second stay in Bath, in 1799, Jane and her family

had stayed with close friends, the Leigh Perrotts, at their home in the Paragon. A wealthy and respected couple, they became involved in a major scandal soon after the Austens left them to return home.

On August 8, 1799 Mr. and Mrs. Leigh Perrott paid a visit to a haberdashers shop run by a Miss Gregory where Mrs. Leigh Perrott bought some black lace that was then wrapped up by the proprietor into a parcel. The Leigh Perrotts left the shop, continued their walk and were just going past the shop once more when Miss Gregory came out and accused Mrs. Leigh Perrott of stealing some white lace. The parcel was opened and much to the Leigh Perrotts' astonishment there were two pieces of lace, one black and one white. There was certainly a suspicion that Miss Gregory had 'planted' the white lace in the hope of getting money from the Leigh Perrotts in return for dropping the charges. If this was the case then the Leigh Perrotts refused to play along. Mrs. Leigh Perrott was eventually charged with attempted larceny and sent to Ilchester Gaol to await trial.

This was not as minor as it appeared. No bail could be allowed on such a charge and the next assizes were a good eight months away. Mrs. Leigh Perrott, aged 60, knew that if found guilty she would face a sentence of 14 years transportation to Australia. The case, on March 29th, 1800, played to a packed audience in the Old Castle Hall, Taunton. After a six hour trial the jury took only a quarter of an hour to return a verdict of 'not guilty', a popular decision by all accounts. Despite their ordeal, the Leigh Perrotts returned to Bath and were instrumental in persuading Mr. Austen to retire there.

In 1806 the Austens moved on to Clifton and then on to Southampton. Let Jane Austen have the last word, writing in 1808:

'It will be two years tomorrow since we left Bath for Clifton, with what happy feelings of Escape!'

Lady Huntingdon's chapel

17. "Attacking Satan at His Headquarters"

Bath has often, to put it mildly, taken a fairly practical view of religion. For instance, when the council bought their first fire-engine in 1741, it was stored in the Abbey. Many inhabitants had no desire to be inconvenienced by the church. When St. James Church was rebuilt in the mid 18th Century, Harrison, the owner of the lower Assembly Rooms, offered to subscribe £200 towards the cost of a new

55

organ; but only as long as the church promised not to annoy him by ringing its bells. With Bath as a fashionable centre for scandal, dancing and gambling, it was no wonder that it was marked out for immediate attention by the new religious group of the 18th Century, the Methodists.

Charles Wesley called it 'attacking Satan at his headquarters'. John Wesley came to Bath on one of his first preaching tours. Four thousand turned up to hear his first sermon, but only a quarter of that number turned up the second time. On the third occasion he had an argument with Beau Nash in which the latter, for once, came off the worse. Worried at the effect on the tourist trade that Wesley might have, Nash struck back. Each time the preacher tried to hold an open air service, Nash would collect an orchestra, reinforced by noisy French horns and kettledrums, to drown him out. For good measure, he made them play 'God save the King', to ensure that the congregation sang along with him. Wesley still managed to have the last word. While walking through Bath one day he came face to face with Nash. The pavement was narrow and one of them would have to step down into the gutter if they were to pass each other. Nash stood his ground: 'I do not give way to fools and knaves!' 'But I do', replied Wesley, and stepped aside.

Neither of these men was a match for the formidable Lady Huntingdon, however, the founder of a particularly austere branch of Methodism and builder of the chapel that still bears her name. She was a most enthusiastic woman; in her younger days, when denied access to the public gallery of the House of Lords, she and her friends showed their displeasure by hammering on the doors for five hours in an attempt to interrupt the Lords' deliberations. On the death of her far from saintly husband, she turned to religion. Many were startled by the change in her. The first visitors to her chapel were, naturally, her upper class friends, many of whom disliked being told that in God's eyes, all men are equal. 'It is monstrous', wrote her friend the Duchess of Buckingham,' to be told that you have a heart as sinful, as the common wretches that crawl the earth.' She took her message to the visitors as well. Once when the Pump Room was full, one of the Society of Friends stood up to talk about the follies and variety of the world. The speech did not go down well in such a place, but the Countess made a point of congratulating the speaker and accompanying her out of the building.

Lady Huntingdon's chapel was often full to capacity and even Nash decided he must pay her a visit to see what was going on. Mindful of public opinion, he was careful to go in secret and only to a small meeting at the Lady's house. But the truth soon came out and once spoof notices began to appear around town advertising the 'Reverend Richard Nash' he became sufficiently embarrassed to drop any further visits.

Other people avoided her for different reasons. It cannot be denied that the Countess could be somewhat overbearing. She wrote to her preachers to point out when they were using 'false doctrine'. Relations were always cool with Wesley who noted her tendency to treat everyone and everything as her private property, 'I mixes with everything – my college, my masters, my students'.

Whatever the truth, Bath did see a rash of local books and pamphlets poking fun at the city's new reputation as a centre of religion. Ridicule had little effect so the critics adopted a new task. As Bath lost its popularity in the 19th Century, the explanation appeared simple: 'nothing thrives in Bath nowadays but preaching and praying'. The clergymen had ruined the place.

18. Squares in the Air

It was in the 18th Century that architects first began to think big and draw up innumerable plans for Bath that never saw

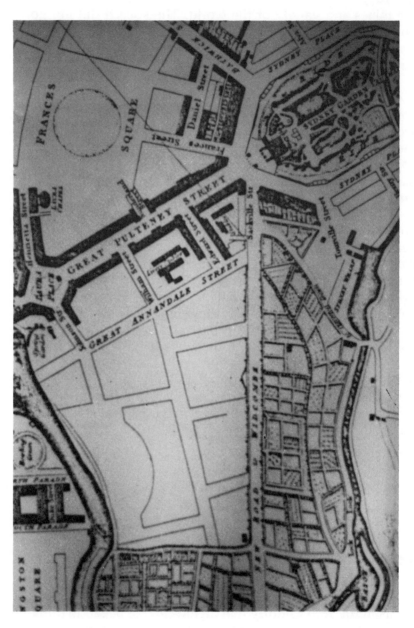

the light of day. Naturally, it was John Wood who had the most far-fetched ideas. Three schemes were put forward. His 'Imperial Gymnasium for the practice of medicinal exercises' never saw the light of day. His Royal Forum got as far as the planning stage. After building North and South Parade, great plans were drawn up for a massive square covering the site of the present Police Station. The name 'Kingston Square' can still be seen overlooking the site in Pierrepont Street, but it was never built.

Wood had more success with his third project, the Grand Circus, although it was never used for the 'Exhibition of Sports' as first intended. Even here, original plans were not adhered to. At first it was meant to be entered via Gay Street with the other two exits terminating in two large houses; but there was great demand for housing and these impressive mansions were scrapped and in place rows of ordinary houses were put up instead to gain more profits. The Circus itself attracted much attention, not all of it favourable. The tiers and decoration reminded one critic of Vespesian's amphitheatre turned inside-out. Others later suggested that after a Circus and the Royal Crescent the Wood family would next produce a star and then all the other constellations in the sky.

The Woods seem to have inspired others to try and emulate them. The Pulteney family had great hopes for their Bathwick lands. William Pulteney had a dream of building a large estate to the east of the city with a wide, impressive road leading over an equally impressive (toll) bridge into Bath. A typically shady deal with the council gave Pulteney land on the city side of the river in return for a promise to build a prison for them on the other side. Pulteney then commissioned the famous designer Robert Adam to design him a bridge. But Adam was famous for interior decoration rather than bridge-building; his shop-lined bridge was far too narrow ever to become a major thoroughfare. Even worse, it began to sink into the river within a few years of completion and major repairs had to be effected.

Undaunted, Adam presented the Pulteney family with grandiose schemes for the Bathwick estate. A massive, wide street would lead out of the city and towards a great circus, some 800 feet across. The Pulteneys seemed to balk at such expensive plans and brought in a new architect, the Town Surveyor Thomas Baldwin, who still hankered after grand schemes. In his plan to the right of Pulteney Street would be a parallel road, Great Annandale Street, and beside it a crescent looking back over the river to the Parade Gardens. To the left would be the gigantic Frances Square. They came to nought. In 1793 threats of invasion during the French revolutionary wars led to a crisis of confidence and a run on the banks bringing all building to an abrupt standstill. Pulteney Street was built but all its grand side-roads exist as mere stumps of plans never completed. Bath Rugby Club now occupy the land earmarked for the crescent.

At the town end of Pulteney Street stands one more site where many ideas have come to grief. The present fountain in Laura Place is fairly recent and replaced a much grander Victorian one (meant, at the time, to be the first of many in Bath). But as soon as the Place was built people had plans to fill the gap in the middle. After Trafalgar some suggested a Nelson's column would look good there. This idea fell through but a column still remained popular and a William IV column was also suggested, to commemorate the Great Reform Bill of 1832. This actually began to be built but as the base was assembled furious locals took matters into their own hands and tore it down: would that similarly inappropriate edifices in Bath had elicited the same enthusiastic response.

In the Victorian period there appear to have been fewer unfulfilled architect's dreams. A version of the Crystal Palace was not erected in Victoria Park. A new Bath college did not appear near Sham Castle, which is probably just as well as its initial prospectus revealed it to be an extreme protestant establishment dedicated to pushing back the rising tide of catholicism. The Victorians were often sucessful because they merely adapted, or expanded, earlier buildings. It was a period when prosperity was at its height and many architects felt all that they needed to do was to plunder the architectural styles of the past. Some fitted in well: in the late

19th Century both the Guildhall and the Pump Room were added to and the joins hardly show. Some ideas are less obvious: in a Roman and Georgian city, I.K. Brunel's railway station is based on a Tudor house and the railway viaduct has medieval castellations. The Victorians were great enthusiasts for the past and were quite ready to improve on their forebears' work. The flying buttresses and tower points on the Abbey are 19th Century: so are the 'Roman' statues around the top of the Great Bath, put there for no other reason than that they looked good and no doubt the Romans would have done the same if they had thought of it first.

It is in the 20th Century though that architects returned to the grand schemes. The Victorians did try to fit in with their surroundings albeit with one or two exceptions such as the Empire Hotel. In this century there has been a return to thinking big and paying little attention to the surroundings. The damage caused by the air-raids in World War II provided a great opportunity which the Abercrombie report of 1945 willingly seized upon. A wholesale rebuilding programme around the centre of Bath would have included the following gems: a new civic centre attached to the rear of the central houses in the Royal Crescent; a major road network running through Julian Road; a Lido on the Recreation Ground; new swimming baths in the Kingsmead area. The plans were too comprehensive – and expensive – ever to stand a real chance of success. The baths would have involved knocking down Kingsmead Flats barely ten years old, for instance. Only a few proposals were adopted piecemeal. A new abattoir in Cheltenham Street, off the Lower Bristol Road, was hardly revolutionary.

The proposed tunnel scheme of the 1960s suffered a similar fate. 'Come to Bath and enjoy the fumes' was a popular sticker at the time. The modern architecture movement did score some successes, if with a fair degree of criticism. The Calton Gardens development was compared to 'Hencoops'; the Beaufort Hotel to a 'Shoe-box.' The crux came when a local firm put forward plans for a new three-storey office block next to the Abbey. Vocal protestors compared it to a 'sugar-cube.' Yehudi Menuhin, then artistic director of

Bath Festival, was dragged in to suggest that they knock down the Empire Hotel and put the new offices up there. A public meeting attracted a wave of apathy. Eleven people turned up to fill the 300 seats alloted to the public. A councillor claimed that most people did not care whether the offices were put up:

> 'There is strong opinion against this project. It is a minority. There is strong opinion in favour. And it is a minority opinion. I feel that in between these two extremes there is a surprisingly large body of opinion who are not extremes, but who are prepared to accept this building in Bath.'

In fact, the company eventually relocated to Manvers Street and the council bought up the threatened buildings next to the Abbey. The argument over the position of modern architecture in Bath continues to rage.

19. Highwaymen and Riotous Fairs

A visit to Bath could sometimes be a risky business. On the outskirts of the city hovered large numbers of highwaymen, foot-pads and common thieves all attracted by the rich pickings and some of them bankrupts who had lost all their money at the gaming tables of Bath.

Claverton Down was notorious for its dangers. Farmers who came to market in Bath would leave for home in company with each other as a form of protection. In March 1753 a Doctor Hancock was held up by two highwaymen who fired a number of shots into his carriage and threatened to shoot his eight-year-old daughter if he did not hand over all his valuables. This was rough treatment, but even worse could

"Only to fire their guns if they were
being attacked"

happen. One Batheaston man had the dubious distinction of being held up three times in two days. Some precautions were taken. John Palmer set up a coach service that travelled very fast and had a guard armed with a blunderbuss. Unfortunately these men tended to get a little enthusiastic as they galloped across the countryside and Palmer had to amend the rules so that the guards were only to fire their guns if they were being attacked.

A more institutionalised form of mayhem was the large number of fairs that appeared in and around the city. One on Broad Quay, near the present Churchill Bridge, was a dangerous place to be on Saturday evening well into this century. On Saturday the Radstock and Peasedown miners would descend on the fair and many a fight would develop between them and the locals. Other fairs did farming business in the daytime but became centres of amusement at night. Holloway fair attracted 'all the thieves and blackguards of the city and its neighbourhood' who would regularly finish an evening by getting fighting drunk and smashing up the booths.

The most notorious fair was at Lansdown but luckily it only occured once a year. Not that the official response to it was always appropriate. In 1808 the local High Constable, Duncan Campbell, decided to take a large number of constables there to try and crack down on the drunkenness and fighting. Soon after he arrived, a drunken brawl broke out between two young men and Campbell stepped in to arrest one of them. The crowd did not approve, scuffled with Campbell and he drew a pistol from his pocket. It failed to fire. The mob moved in further, Campbell drew another pistol which unfortunately did work and a man fell dead. The crowd howled for blood, Campbell turned tail and fled to a friend's house in Lansdown Crescent. The luckless lawman was brought to trial on a charge of manslaughter. He must have had friends in high places: found guilty, he had to pay a £5 fine and serve a mere three months imprisonment.

The Lansdown fairs continued and the conduct got no better. In 1839 there was a full-scale battle. As the stallholders were clearing up late one night, there arrived a whole horde of slum dwellers from the city led by one 'Carroty Kate' an infamous local character, as vicious as any man with a habit of wandering around half naked. The stallholders could do nothing as the locals smashed up the booths and seized all the alcohol, drinking themselves into a stupor. This was to prove their undoing however. As they staggered off home in the early dawn, the fairmen gathered together, armed themselves with clubs and waited to pick up the stragglers. Kate and some twelve of her followers were cornered by thirty of the stall-holders at the bottom of Lansdown Hill. Gleefully the fairmen took their revenge. Kate's followers were tied up with rope and dragged through a nearby pond, time and time again until some were unconscious. Then for good measure they were tied to cart-wheels and whipped. Kate, being a woman, was not ducked in the pond. She was merely tied to a cart-wheel and caned by other women from the fair.

Others of the raiders were intercepted by the police and a running battle developed between the two sides, a number of men being crippled for life. And Kate? She survived her treatment, and was seen to crawl away swearing revenge. The records did not reveal whether she fulfilled this threat.

20. Rebellion at Bath

Few people choose to be on the losing side in any struggle; unfortunately it is not always easy to work out who will triumph in the end. The mid 1680s were a particularly bad time for local authorities, most of them dependent for their positions on the King, for there was great confusion as to who should hold this highest position in the land. James II was the rightful ruler but many people disliked him and in his short reign he faced two revolts, one led by his illegitimate nephew, the Duke of Monmouth, and the second by his eldest daughter, Mary, and her Dutch husband, William. Thus James, Monmouth and Mary were all potential rulers; and Bath was visited by all three.

James became King in 1685; Bath corporation was one of the first to send messages of goodwill to him. But almost immediately there was a crisis as Monmouth landed in the west country and headed for Bath. He had arrived too early, before James had proved he could be a bad King, and only a few people flocked to his banner. When Monmouth arrived outside Bath the corporation prudently closed the gates on him. The duke sent one of his men forward to parley with the local inhabitants but, rather unsportingly, they shot him dead. Monmouth soon retired south and to eventual defeat.

But the rebellion was not over yet. James sent the infamous Judge Jefferies to root out rebel supporters and he rarely gave anyone the benefit of the doubt. Bath had ignored Monmouth, but the Judge still managed to find six inhabitants guilty and they were sentenced to death. Jefferies took a keen interest in their fate and sent a detailed letter to Bath council demanding that they be hung, drawn and quartered. In it, he asked for faggots to burn their bowels, a furnace to boil their heads and quarters and sufficient spears and poles to stick them upon. 'You are also to provide an axe and a cleaver for the quartering of the said rebels' he reminded them: a thorough approach to crime and punishment to say the least.

Few escaped Jefferies and not all were guilty. Near Bath, in the village of Norton St. Philip, the Judge reputedly set up a temporary court in the 'George Inn'. As usual, a fair number of men were sentenced to death. They were to be hanged in an orchard nearby, which involved them walking through a passageway in another pub, the 'Fleur de Lys'. As they walked along, a stranger to the area who was drinking in the pub held a gate open for them. The condemned men walked through but as the stranger made to close the gate one of the guards stopped him, thinking he was one of the prisoners. Despite his protests he was hanged along with the others. The ghost of this unfortunate good Samaritan is still said to haunt the passageway.

Monmouth himself was eventually executed as well. James became more unpopular the longer he ruled but most people felt that they could put up with him as his successor

The George Inn, Norton St Philip

would be his Protestant daughter, Mary, and James' wife was seen as unable to have any more children. Then in summer 1687 James brought his wife, Mary of Modena, to Bath to take the waters. The city had long claimed that the waters could increase fertility; whatever the truth of this tale,

Mary astonished everyone by giving birth the following year. She had a baby boy, who would now take precedence over his elder sister Mary. Bath sent its congratulations but many people felt this was the last straw: James' son might be as bad a king as he was. Thus just when Bath was proclaiming its loyalty, and thinking to itself that its waters may have had some part in the happy event, many others were beginning to plot to get rid of James.

Leading politicians invited William and Mary to come over from the Netherlands. William, like Monmouth, arrived in the south-west but that was the only similarity with the luckless Duke. By now most were annoyed with James and even his senior army commander, John Churchill, deserted to the other side. James eventually fled the country without a fight. Bath was one of the first cities to send the new King and Queen their congratulations.

The slums of Bath

21. Beggars and Beatings

In 1597, under Queen Elizabeth I, an act was passed that inadvertently turned Bath into a mecca for the poor and made the phrase 'The Beggars of Bath' famous throughout the country. The act meant well. It said that Bath's healing waters should be made use of by all those who needed them and in particular the 'diseased and impotent poor'. Parishes were encouraged to contribute towards the exercise of sending their most needy cases to the spa town – and few needed any second bidding. The Poor Law of the time stated that the needy had to be supported by the parish in which they were resident: so crafty parishes encouraged their beggars to go to Bath and settle there, ridding them of the cost of looking after them. Bath council, having to keep the baths open to all, could not refuse them.

Clearly this was a situation that Bath did not want to continue and in the early 18th Century the council managed to have the Elizabethan legislation repealed: the baths were no longer 'open house' to the poor of the whole of England. But the city was still full of rich pickings and the beggars were not to be put off so easily. They merely moved outside the limits of the council's jurisdiction, which meant a very short distance indeed. The council's writ extended little further than the limits of the old medieval walls, so the poor just decamped over the river to the south and east of the town and the council could not touch them.

As a result the areas of Holloway and Widcombe became notorious for the behaviour of their inhabitants and places to be avoided by polite society. Holloway was known for its beggars and its ill-kept donkeys (used for bringing coal from the Somerset pits to Bath). The Dolemeads, an area to the east of the city, was a 'perfect colony of vice and dissipation,' not helped by the fact that it was so low-lying that the river flooded over it with monotonous regularity. In the mid 19th Century the local vicar estimated that 60% of the inhabitants were on the poverty line and it was rumoured that North Parade Bridge was built partly to allow people to leave the city without having to pass through the Dolemeads. In the early 1900s the authorities raised the ground level of the entire area by some thirteen feet and in typical optimistic fashion gave the roads new and bright sounding names, Excelsior Street for example, but this still did not do much for the area.

At least by that time most of the beggars had gone. For much of the 18th and 19th Centuries they headed into the city by day and retreated back to the hovels come the night. If caught for any minor misdemeanour, the punishment could be severe. Stocks and a pillory stood near the old Guildhall (near the site of the present one) and it was not just rotten fruit that was thrown at them: mud, eggs, fish entrails and other objects hit the helpless victims who, for good measure, might also be flogged until the blood ran down their backs. A variant on this activity was to flog the culprit from the Market Place to the Old Bridge – i.e. until he reached the river to the south and the safety of Widcombe. The villain was usually given a few seconds start and the whole affair was very much a public spectacle. Women were treated a little better; they only had to run half the distance.

This rather barbaric treatment still took place in the early years of the 19th Century, but the times were changing and the punishments becoming less severe. Finally, in 1834 the council took the logical step and extended the city boundaries to include the slum areas over the river. Within three years the local inhabitants were complaining of the excessive number of police in the Widcombe area, a sure sign that things were improving there.

The same could not be said for an area nearer the centre, and that was Kingsmead. For years the most notorious area of the city was that centred on Avon Street down by the river. Built in the early 1700s, it was never a success, due largely to the fact that it was very low-lying and flooded almost every year. The rich moved out, the prostitutes moved in. So infamous was the area that the more adventurous of the genteel society of Georgian times would, after dinner, go for a walk down the street to view their poorer brethren. At times a new mayor would begin his period in office by sending in the police to arrest everyone in the street thus causing great embarassment to those curious souls unlucky enough to be sight-seeing that night.

By 1800 Avon Street was already famous as the 'receptacle for fallen women,' and all respectable people gave it a wide berth: in Jane Austen's 'Persuasion' one impoverished character lives too close to the area for Sir Walter Elliot's comfort. By 1821 it was estimated that one third of families living in the street were unmarried and one quarter of the children were illegitimate. This was one of the places where beggars would stand at the end of the road in the hope of being knocked down by passing wagons so that they could claim compensation.

Regular flooding not only brought damp and misery but also the threat of disease. Flood waters pushed sewerage up from the inadequate drainage system and in the 1830s when 49 people died of cholera in one year, 27 of these came from Avon Street. The situation cannot have been helped by the fact that the council of Bath, in attempting to stem this outbreak, refused to allow cholera sufferers into the city but directed them all to one allocated house: in Avon Street.

The area became so poor that even the prostitutes eventually moved out followed soon after by the large numbers of public houses. In 1880 a newspaper report on an election meeting noted the arrival of a gang of Avon Street men armed with thick sticks. Their reputation preceded them: their arrival was greeted with 'overpowering groans'. Nor did they fail to live up to expectations and several sharp fights soon broke out.

In the 1930s the council levelled the entire area and earmarked the Avon Street site for a new hospital. The war brought these plans to a temporary halt and in its own way caused further confusion. The flattened area appeared in German propaganda photos after the air-raids as an area destroyed by their bombing. This zone of longtime dubious distinction is now a car park.

22. Turning the Tables

In its heyday, huge fortunes could be made at cards. It was claimed that Midford Castle, near Bath, was built in the shape of the Ace of Clubs to commemorate the fact that its costs were met by profits from gambling. Sir Philip Francis was said to have won £20,000 in one night (although in polite society, you might be shunned the next day for doing rather too well). Some doctors in Bath recommended gambling as a means of relaxing and an aid to your treatment at the waters; but many accounts of the time show that it was not always as genteel as it appeared to be.

The city was infested with those who would prey on the innocent visitor. Loaded dice were in abundance. Card 'sharps' would play with marked cards. 'Rooks' hovered in the background at the gambling saloons, ever ready to lend money to those doing badly who were convinced that one more round and their luck would turn. Then, next morning, the 'rook' would arrive at the luckless gambler's lodgings to claim back the loan with exorbitant rates of interest. Some never even made it to the gambling tables; disreputable saloons would wine and dine young men and strip them of all their valuables once they had drunk themselves insensible. Other card sharps would turn their attentions to the ladies, finding the innocent daughters of the rich and offering to marry them. At least one young lady was 'snatched' by sedan chairmen hired by one frustrated hardened gambler. Another girl would have gone willingly if Nash had not caught wind of the scheme and tipped the mother off: she left the Assembly Rooms early and thus arrived home in time to foil the elopement.

There was also one much-publicised incident in which Nash showed the evils gambling held for the innocent. A newly married couple came to Bath for their honeymoon. The husband began to gamble, became obsessed with it and threatened to become bankrupt. Nash hired a professional player to clear him out in double quick time; and then han-

ded back all the money when he saw that the young man
had learned his lesson. Others were less fortunate and could
not live with the shame of being penniless. One unsuccess-
ful player hanged himself at the 'Bear' inn; a youth shot
himself in the head; at least one noble lady did away with
herself. If people realised they were being cheated, they
often made a fight of it. At least one detected cheat was
thrown out of a first floor window. Another who seemed to
be a little too agile with his fingers, had his hand pinned to

73

the table with a fork, his opponent making the gentlemanly observation 'Sir, if you have not a card under that hand, I apologise.' Many an argument ended in a duel: the last official one, before Nash banned them, being between two professional gamblers that ended with one of them being run through by the other's sword.

Nash was hardly blameless himself. He made his money by taking a cut from the profits of those rooms to which he introduced customers. But the times were changing and public attitudes were hardening against gambling. In 1739 an act was passed banning certain named card games; so Bath just changed their names and continued as before. A new act banned all card games and all number games such as roulette; so Nash introduced EO, a roulette game with 'Even' and 'Odd' letters around the wheel. Finally the government banned most gambling games outright. The gambling fraternity went underground. Thus the authorities had to seek them out. In early January 1750 the mayor and corporation of Bath descended on one house near Westgate acting on a tip-off. In a darkened upstairs room, sixteen men were found at an illegal EO table. Two jumped out the window but one misjudged his leap and was killed. The table was thrown out after him, to be hacked to pieces and burnt.

By this time, Nash was on the way out as well. He had demanded a 50% cut of the profits from Wiltshire's assembly rooms. Wiltshire refused, claiming this was too much. With a certain lack of forethought, Nash took the case to court but the law was no longer on his side. The transaction was deemed invalid because it was immoral, Nash lost popularity for the way he got his money, and for good measure, Wiltshire was fined £500 for keeping an unlawful gaming table.

23. Rhymes Without Reason

It is not that Bath has produced few top rank poets that are worthy of note; after all, not many places can boast famous writers of any description. No, what has been commented on by weary observers is the fact that Bath has produced so many truly awful poets who have felt the need to put their feelings about the city into print.

There have been a few exceptions, but hardly first-rate ones. Walter Savage Landor wrote poetry but unfortunately his work included rather disrespectful ditties about the then King, George IV, which did not do much to further his career. Christopher Anstey actually managed to achieve posthumous fame by being buried in Poets Corner in Westminster Abbey but his greatest work, the 'New Bath Guide', was a gentle dig at the city. It ended with the hero penniless, the heroine let down by her suitor and the two supporting females deceived by, respectively, a Moravian preacher and an hypocritical Methodist. It was a bestseller and encouraged a new trend (endless Postscripts to the New Bath Guide and others attempting to cash in) but it was hardly great poetry. Even some more famous poets seem to have been other than inspired in their visits to the city: Cowpers 'Verses written at Bath on finding the Heel of a Shoe' is not the most exciting title of all time.

Even more depressing was the fact that so many ordinary people were inspired by the waters to burst into verse. Nicknamed the 'Water Poets' these enthusiastic visitors stuck to a number of subjects that were depressingly similar: love either enkindled by the waters and leading to happiness or love over-excited by the waters and leading to death. Others, with an eye to profit, would churn out pieces of gushing praise concerning any beautiful, or at least rich, women that happened to be in the city at the time.

Such writers were determined to inflict their works on the general public and many would pay to print a limited run of their works in the hope that they would be snapped up by an eager audience. The most famous local author whose ambitions were greater than her talents was a Mrs. Miller who went as far as to organise fortnightly poetry competitions. Her life was normal enough until she went with her husband on a grand tour around Europe. Fired with enthusiasm, she returned to her home in Batheaston with a vase that she had picked up in Italy, said to have once belonged to the famous Roman, Cicero. This led her to start her competitions. A select gathering would be given a specific topic (not all of the highest order: buttered muffins was one chosen subject) and have fourteen days to produce a six line poem or 'bout rimé' on that theme. On the chosen day the contestants would return to Mrs. Miller's house, deposit their poems in the vase and the have them read out aloud. The gentlemen would retire into the house to eat, drink and choose the best three. Mrs. Miller would then personally hand out the prizes: a bouquet of flowers to the winner down to a sprig of myrtle to the third placed.

The contestants were often a very carefully chosen group of the titled and famous; but none were famous for writing poetry and the collections that were published, containing a rather large proportion of poems by Mrs. Miller herself, were universally drab. Even so, the first volume sold out in two days although this was probably because the writers were well known rather than for the intrinsic value of the poems themselves. Mrs. Miller certainly enjoyed herself: the competitions ran for a good twelve years. But enthusiasm rather than ability remained the order of the day: 'Tis a very diminutive principality with large pretensions' as Walpole put it.

24. Things That go Bump in the Night

Not all ghost stories are as they first appear; John Wood's 18th Century tale of a neighbour of his has quite an unexpected ending.

A wealthy Quaker gentleman took possession of a house in St. John's Court and put a trusted woman servant in charge. All went well at first but then in the early days of December 1733 the woman began to complain of strange noises that could be heard coming from just outside the house. Each night as she lay down to sleep, the noises would begin. Convinced the house was haunted, she decided to leave.

Her master was not particularly sympathetic. As a religious man he was quite adamant that 'infernal spirits' and the like could not exist. On a more mundane level, he also had no wish for the house to gain the reputation of being haunted. He decided to sleep in the servant woman's bedroom and see for himself what was going on. The next evening he moved his bed, himself and his wife into the haunted room.

Things did not go quite as planned. Just as the couple was drifting off to sleep, the noises began and they continued throughout the night. The two spent a night of absolute terror, so frightened, as Wood put it, that they 'grossly offended their sheets'. In the morning the Quaker gentleman turned for help; he invited three Church of England clergymen to come round and put the ghost down.

Meanwhile the gossips had been at work. There were already rumours as to who the ghost was and where he had come from. It was claimed that it was the ghost of a coloured man who had been a loyal servant to a sea captain who had formerly lived in the house and had died in the very room that was said to be haunted. On his death bed the captain had given his servant over to the care of the Quaker gentle-

"The two spent a night of absolute
terror"

man who now owned the house. But a substantial amount of money was also left to the servant, according to the gossips, and person or persons unknown had taken the money, killed the servant and handed his body over to be cut up by the medical profession. The servant's spirit, seeking vengeance, was supposed to have taken the form of a giant mastiff hound.

Whether the Quaker gentleman heard this rather scandalous rumour is unknown, but the story soon became common knowledge; so much so that in fact on the evening of 12 December 1733, when the three clergymen were to lay the ghost, a veritable army of ghost-hunters and fashionable folk turned up to see what was going to happen. The Quaker let them in and they all sat quietly until 2 a.m. when a violent quarrel broke out between the owner of the house and one of the guests. The rest of the people there watched with great amusement and the party broke up soon afterwards with many professing themselves well content with the evening even though no ghost had been sighted or heard.

The Quaker now returned to his first suspicion, that there was no ghost. The next night, the only inhabitant of the house was William Fraser, a burly labourer, armed with an oak cudgel and instructions to knock any potential visitor on the head.

Nothing happened that night. Undaunted, Fraser returned the next evening. This time there was much more going on. As darkness fell the noises were heard again, louder than ever. A blast of wind outside shattered windows, smashed roofs and sent slates, tiles and glass flying across the streets. Superstitious watchers claimed that this was the revenge of the 'Inhabitants of the Infernal Regions' who were looking rather askance at the prospect of one of their number being hit by a cudgel. Luckily, Fraser was made of stronger stuff. Looking around the 'haunted' room he noticed that the small shutter to one window was tied too loosely and this was the simple explanation for all the strange noises. When the wind blew from a particular direction and all the doors in the house were closed, then the loose shutter made all the 'strange' noises that had been heard.

Fraser tightened the string holding the shutter and thus laid the ghost.

First published in Great Britain by
ASHGROVE PRESS LIMITED
19, Circus Place, Bath, Avon BA1 2PW

Rothnie, Niall
    Unknown Bath: scandals and secrets from
    the past.
    1. Bath (Avon) — History   2. Bath
    (Avon) — Moral conditions
    l. Title
    942.3'98   DA690.B3
    ISBN 0-906798-68-X

Photoset in Palatino by
Spire Print Services, Salisbury
Printed in Great Britain by
Bath Midway Litho Ltd., Bath, Avon